"Ha Jin ... is a writer of simple yet powerful gifts."
—*The New York Times*

"Ha Jin profoundly understands the conflict
between the individual and society, between the
timeless universality of the human heart and
constantly shifting politics of the moment. With
wisdom, restraint, and empathy ... he vividly reveals
the complexities and subtleties of a world ... we
desperately need to know."
—Judges' citation, National Book Award

A Distant Center

CopperCanyonPress.org

BUSINESS REPLY MAIL
FIRST-CLASS MAIL   PERMIT NO. 43   PORT TOWNSEND WA

POSTAGE WILL BE PAID BY ADDRESSEE

Copper Canyon Press
PO Box 271
Port Townsend, WA 98368-9931

What do you think?

BOOK TITLE: _____

COMMENTS: _____
_____
_____

OUR MISSION:

Poetry is vital to language and
living. Copper Canyon Press
publishes extraordinary poetry
from around the world to
engage the imaginations and
intellects of readers.

Thank you for your thoughts!

Can we quote you? ☐ yes ☐ no

☐ Please send me a catalog full of poems and email news on forthcoming
titles, readings, and poetry events.

☐ Please send me information on becoming a patron of Copper Canyon Press.

NAME: _____

ADDRESS: _____

CITY: _____ STATE: _____ ZIP: _____

EMAIL: _____

MAIL THIS CARD, SHARE YOUR COMMENTS ON FACEBOOK OR TWITTER,
OR EMAIL POETRY@COPPERCANYONPRESS.ORG

詩 Copper Canyon Press
A nonprofit publisher dedicated to poetry

HA JIN

A Distant Center

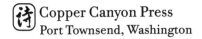
Copper Canyon Press
Port Townsend, Washington

Cover art: *Home within Home within Home within Home within Home,* 2013, polyester fabric, metal frame, 1,530 × 1,283 × 1,297 cm, site-specific commissioned artwork for Hanjin Shipping Box Project MMCA (National Museum of Modern and Contemporary Art), Seoul, 13 November 2013– 11 May 2014. © Do Ho Suh

Copper Canyon Press is in residence at Fort Worden State Park in Port Townsend, Washington, under the auspices of Centrum. Centrum is a gathering place for artists and creative thinkers from around the world, students of all ages and backgrounds, and audiences seeking extraordinary cultural enrichment.

LIBRARY OF CONGRESS CATALOGING-IN-PUBLICATION DATA

Names: Jin, Ha, 1956– author.
Title: Distant center / Ha Jin.
Description: Port Townsend, Washington : Copper Canyon Press, [2017]
Identifiers: LCCN 2017037820 | ISBN 9781556594625 (hardcover)
Classification: LCC PS3560.I6 A6 2018 | DDC 811/.54–dc23
LC record available at https://lccn.loc.gov/2017037820

9 8 7 6 5 4 3 2 FIRST PRINTING

Copper Canyon Press
Post Office Box 271
Port Townsend, Washington 98368

www.coppercanyonpress.org

For Lisha

CONTENTS

vii

A Distant Center

A Solitary Traveler

YOU MUST NOT RUN IN PLACE

Don't say since life is short and precarious,
you want to live effortlessly.
Don't brag you will try to outsmart time –
every day you'll watch movies and eat dim sum
while chatting idly with friends.

Better keep busy like the others
who work for a sack of rice or a set of clothes.
See how steady those footsteps are on the wharf,
look at the ships leaving the port –
heavy, they are still going far.

THE LONG-DISTANCE TRAVELER

Keep going: the farther you go,
the smaller you grow
in the eyes of those
who can't walk anymore, until one day they can
no longer see you. Then
they will declare that you
have disappeared, that
your foolish choice will reduce you
to a lonely ghost in the wilderness.

Keep going, don't turn to look back.
Always carry enough food and water
and follow no one's map
but your own. May you have
fresh excitement every day, but don't
linger at any charming site for long. If you are
blazing a path, do not expect to meet
a fellow traveler. If by chance
you go astray, you will still
have the sun and stars.

THE DETACHED

Still I praise those who are detached
from any land, who, since birth,
have been determined to travel far in search
of home. They get their bearings
by stars, their roots growing at the end
of the imagined sky.

For them, life is a tortuous journey
and every stop a new departure. They
know they will disappear on the road,
but as long as they are living,
death keeps them company
to the destination they have envisioned,
though they have no idea
whose maps their footprints might update.

DIFFICULTIES

Don't mention your loss again.
Indeed, you've lost so many things:
home, jobs, family, a country.
You landed in such a place
where everything is strange,
where you must start all over.
Sometimes you are like a child
who has just begun to talk,
sometimes you are like an old woman,
confused, unable to collect yourself.
These years you have lived
from loss to loss to loss,
surrounded by difficulties.

But whose life, if meaningful,
is not rooted in a predicament
and made of difficulties?
Stop talking about suffering.
Sufferings are never equal –
compared to billions of people,
you ought to feel fortunate
that you can start again.

TALENT

How many people wish you were mediocre
so as to prove you are the same as they?
Now that you want to stand out,
you will have to endure pain and injury –
surely there will be fists that all at once
hit you from different directions.
But even if a whole gang attacks you
you mustn't fight back, because
they mean to sidetrack you
and watch you rolling in mud.

Keep in mind your talent also includes
patience and endurance.
Get up, move quietly, and leave
all the clamor behind.

MISFORTUNE

Misfortune is again descending.
In what fashion will it appear this time?
You have seen calamities and deaths
and have been shaken by shattered families,
their members scattered everywhere.

So many times you almost collapsed,
moaning, "No more – I'm done for!"
But you picked yourself up
and set out again, although
you had to make abrupt turns,
had to cross new hills and valleys
learning another kind of staggering.

Now, misfortune is coming,
but you don't tremble anymore,
already familiar with its company:
beneath a ghastly mask are the faces
of various deities, including Opportunity.

THE CHOICE OF EXILE

Although you are almost middle-aged
you still want to uproot yourself
and go far away so you can start over.
You haven't set out yet, uncertain
where to put down roots.

You often wish you could be like that artist
who bought a little island so that
he could live freely on his own land.
He raised vegetables and chickens, did carpentry,
planted bamboo and fruit trees
all over the slope beyond his cottage.
Every season was like spring on his island,
where he could hear only the tides and birdsong.
It was beautiful and quiet enough to smother him.

Don't forget he chose to kill himself
and even strangled his wife,
because he couldn't see how to continue,
so crushed was he by madness and fear.

From the very beginning he should have known
that if he chose exile he would have no land of his own
– the desire to depart
would rise in him again and again –
he could find no home other than the road.

Don't dream of taking root somewhere else.
Once you start out, you must live like a boat,
accepting a wandering fate
drifting from port to port, to port…

A 58-YEAR-OLD PAINTER LEAVING FOR AMERICA

Tomorrow you will leave Shanghai,
the city you used to love,
to look for another life far away.
"Probably another death,"
you often joke with a smile these days.

You have attempted death several times.
Expel it from your mind.
No matter how hard life is there,
you must continue to live.
As long as you are alive
there will be miracles.

Indeed, you have no English
or youth for starting over,
only your paintbrush and fortitude.
In that strange land
you must live, as always,
with stubbornness and care.

You must quit drinking and avoid
staying up all night.
Keep in mind the meaning of
your existence: wherever you land,
your footprints will become milestones.

IN SASKATCHEWAN

Facing a thousand acres for sale,
your cheeks turn pink, your eyes flashing.
True, if you pay a hundred thousand dollars,
this farm will be yours,
together with the pasture and the farmhouse.

I know you are a farmer's granddaughter.
Your family's land was confiscated
by the state during the land reform,
but in your veins still flows
the hunger for sowing and harvesting.
How you long to live like your friend,
the one from Henan province –
she put down roots here, raised
a family, followed daylight
to go to work and returned to rest,
busy or relaxing according to the season.
Your friend's farm extends to the end of the sky,
already over ten thousand acres.
She has her own forest and lake.

Heavens – this makes me envious, too!
But don't forget you are destined to wander.
Your home is on the road, and on paper.
You used to say that most property
was merely extra fat.

THE ROADS I TRAVELED

I tried to throw off all the roads I had traveled,
but by chance I brought a few with me.
Now, wherever I go, I can feel them
stretching away under my feet,
though I have no idea how they continue
to join or cross new roads.

But I am already clear about this:
all the new roads stem from
the journeys I once made.
Perhaps someday I can say with pride
that my old paths have
led me into new terrains.

MISSING HOME

Homesickness is a deep heartache, even
though you no longer know where home is.
Home is an existence of another kind –
once lost, it can't be recovered
except in your thought and memory.

The swirling leaves can make one sad,
but you are used to the late autumn scene.
The trees will sprout green next spring.
There's no need to feel so blue now.

Nowadays so many homes rise in your mind,
all in places you have never been.
Your dreams of the future and your longing
for the past are nothing but fantasies
of how to stop being a stranded traveler.

CEMETERY

I have seen the beauty of that cemetery,
where grassy slopes glow with sunshine
and the North Atlantic tides lap
at the pebbles and granite steps.
Tombstones spread from winding paths,
where Mexican workers trim flowers.
It's so peaceful and sunny everywhere,
and everything is neatly organized.
I can see why both of you want to go there
and even purchased plots for your families
who have yet to leave our motherland.

Knowing where to end can help
to curb your wandering heart
and stabilize this drifting life.
In fact, a fine cemetery is a village
or town of another kind, where
people can settle afterward.
I envy your clarity about your journey's end,
but I'm still not sure where to go,
never attached to any place.
Even after this life, I might continue to roam.

Missed Time

MISSED TIME

after Dai Wangshu

My notebook has remained blank for months
thanks to the light you shower
around me. I have no use
for my pen, which lies
languorously without grief.

Nothing is better than to live
a storyless life that needs
no writing for meaning –
when I am gone, let others say
they lost a happy man,
though no one can tell how happy I was.

FIRE

They all avoided the smoke.
Only you, from far away,
saw the fire smoldering in me.
Quietly you came over
and hugged me as if to keep warm,
saying, "Like this forever."

Only you, only you
can bear the raging fire.
It's burning only for you
so you can live a life of splendor,
not afraid of cold even in deep winter.
Every month will pass like a day.

LULLABY

Sleep well, sweetheart.
You were busy the whole day –
you tidied up our home, went shopping,
picked up the mail at the post office,
mended our fence, cooked,
and paid all the monthly bills.

Sleep well, sweetheart.
I'm staying beside you,
relishing the time we are together.
The flowers in our yard are blooming
and the rabbits and groundhogs
have returned to their burrows.

Sleep well, sweetheart.
Beyond the window the moon is large and round.
There are no furious cries
or fearsome faces here.
Tonight you must sleep peacefully
so you will wake to another good day.

AGAIN, SPEAKING OF THOSE I ONCE LOVED

They all longed to have a home,
but I could only promise to try my best
to let them live comfortably.
If they were afraid of ice and snow
we'd go south of the Yangtze.
If they didn't like a humid climate
we would move to a plain or plateau.

But they all kept an eye on the present,
eager for an actual home:
a spacious apartment that had better
have a shower and a balcony.

Only you said everything
didn't have to come all at once
as long as we could often be
together – especially on holidays –
at least I should be home for the Spring Festival.
You hoped that uneventful days
would follow one another without pause.

Now we have our house, our lawn and woods,
the moonlight on our driveway white like frost.
Turkeys and deer frequent our backyard.
But none of these could make a home
without your nurturing.

A VISITOR

Again snow covers New England.
There will be no school tomorrow
and we won't go to work.
At night trucks drone
on the distant roads,
spraying sand and salt.
More snow brings more business
to the plowing workers –
it's their season of harvest.

This morning I open my curtains
and find footprints scattered in my yard.
They were left behind by a deer,
who must have lingered here for a long time.

Again I think of you.
You often said you'd go to Florida
where there is a lot of sunlight
and no snow. Now you have gone
to another place where
there is no winter or storm,
though I'm not sure whether you are lonesome.

THE ONE FOLLOWING YOU

Because of you, that coastal city
has appeared on my map.
In my mind it's no longer
a fishing village far away.

Every morning I wake
to follow you on the bus to work,
past the bay enclosed in mist
and through a long tunnel into town.
We then walk along the street shaded by maples,
enter a gate to a schoolhouse,
and finally stand before a room of children.
You open a textbook and read to them
legends of triumph and updated fables.
You also draw on the chalkboard
a tomorrow that might be more colorful.

Whether you know it or not,
whether you like it or not,
you always bring along
an invisible guard.

SURPRISE

Don't strain your mind
to produce another surprise for her.
Love, won that way, is hard to sustain
and soon you'll find yourself exhausted.
More terrible, someday
you might be disgusted with yourself,
feeling you have wasted your life
without achieving anything.

Above all, you mustn't lose your bearings.
Don't follow others to seek
excitement or a so-called quality life.
What's invaluable in love is to help
each other reach the end of a long road.
Although every day seems the same,
love resides in the ordinary.

AN IDEAL LIFE

How I long for an unoccupied life.
I can sleep in on weekdays,
then go to Starbucks to read newspapers
and chat with friends, cracking jokes.
There's no need to hurry to work
or analyze the smiles
of my boss and clients,
though people say I'm too lazy,
staying home all the time and kept by my wife.

I often ask myself:
why must I be the mainstay
of my household? I struggle
outside in the world. I try to serve
my children, satisfy my wife.

You don't have to live so hard.
You don't need to carry on your bloodline.
You can live with ease and die
alone, at your own pace.

But at night I often hear a voice
whisper, tickling my ear:
"There's no meaning in an effortless life –
you came into this world
just to strive into another self."

TWO IMAGES

In my dreams you wear the army
uniform, a belt, and knee-high boots.
Your pair of short braids jumps a little
as you stride around fearlessly.
In a husky voice you give orders
while shells burst like blossoms far away.
People say you are a born general.

In reality you look like an elegant lady.
Your lilac skirt floats across
the quiet plaza before a church.
Your heels knock the stone slabs
washed glossy by a spring shower.
Your voice is the wings of doves
waving in the sunshine.
Your figure draws so many admiring eyes.

Which one of them are you –
a fierce officer or a refined lady?
I hope you are neither.

APRIL

Again it's the season when
the new and the old are both
trembling. From the lake in the woods
come fits of frogs' cries
together with scattered birdcalls
and the shedding of rotted branches and bark.

You used to say that before
the spring you would send me
a garden of blossoms. Now
winter is gone, but for you,
spring is still an ocean away.

Home on the Road

A SNOWSTORM

Three feet of snow covers the north,
bringing five states to a standstill:
stores, schools, airports, all are closed.
Only plow trucks fill the streets.
At last we can stay home for a day.

Yesterday before leaving work
we wished each other a peaceful break:
Be careful when you dig out —
don't hurt your back or arms.
We're grateful to the bad weather
that allows us a day's rest.

But it's not yet eight in the morning
and my phone begins to ring.
So many calls keep coming in,
fundraising or telemarketing:
a foundation for children's education,
a breast cancer research institute,
a veterans' service center,
a wireless company, an insurance agency,
even the fire station and town police who are
doing a survey of the residents.

Heavens, so many people busy themselves
unwilling to take a break.

A NEW HOPE

Yesterday at noon we stopped
at the square to bother
the fat snowman, twisting his nose,
a big carrot, and poking his eyes,
a pair of batteries. Each of us slapped him
a couple of times, to break his heart
so he wouldn't dare come to Boston again,
would take away the snowbanks
that were almost 6 feet high.

But this morning the TV announced
that it has snowed 102 inches to date –
with 5 more inches, it will break the record.
All of a sudden we got excited again,
chatting about the imminent snowstorm
and hoping it will be heavy enough.

IN THE SPRINGTIME

Still you should praise the spring,
although it's a miserable season
for you. It revives the memories
that never die –
all the fields to be sown,
the endless sweating with painful limbs,
sleeping with clothes on at night,
rising before daybreak
to follow others to welcome a dry spring
with a hoe or a shoulder pole.

Here spring is another sight.
On the town green
toddlers wave their plump arms,
the white soles of their feet following
pigeons and geese on the grass.
But whenever you go out
you can't stop sneezing,
your eyes itchy with tears,
your nose red and swollen.
Only through a window can you watch
the kids and their mothers at play.

In the kitchen the radio is loud.
The show host has been talking happily
with callers, so many of them phoning in
to praise such a gorgeous day.
True, your body rejects this spring,
but still you must learn to praise.
Praise everything burgeoning with life,
the worms that come out for sunlight,

the pollen that gives you hay fever,
the snails drunk with rainwater,
the houses that begin to take shape.

TOADS

You ought to admire the toads' vitality.
In a stream or a sewer
they can live, often wild with joy.
In the early spring they croak with gusto,
giving you the illusion that large flocks
of ducks and geese are paddling nearby.

Look, they leap around
like little birds attempting flight,
though they have no wings.
Neither do they have a waist,
but they all swagger when they walk.
If they sit, they look like ministatues
of Buddha, too dignified to rise.
In fact, they can never stand up.

A TUG OF WAR

Little wren, I know you love
the eaves above my door,
but you can't build here.

You trash the place
and even shit on the door handle,
soiling my hand again.

Again I sweep away your embryo
of a nest. You'll return
to restart your project.

Little rascal, I won't let you
pile mud and grass here.
Even friends cannot share everything.

There are eaves everywhere.
Why are you so determined
to settle above my door?

COPYING CHARACTERS

See, here're your brush and copybook.
From now on you must practice calligraphy –
copy four or five pages every day.
You must be able not just to speak Chinese
but also to inscribe it.
Handsome handwriting
ensures a bright future.

Every weekend you make me
go to the Chinese school.
I need more time for my homework in
science and history and also
have to read novels and plays in English.
I have no time for copying characters.
If you go on distracting me like this,
I might have to repeat seventh grade.

Don't give us such an excuse.
You must inscribe characters more often.
Once you start something
you must see it through.
If you cannot write Chinese,
you will be like a disabled person
when we go back to live in Tianjin.

Now I can see why Chinese
are so good at making knockoffs.
A couple of guys at my school
always copy characters at home.
In every class they can't stop
copying each other's homework.

I don't want to be like those copycats
who have practiced duplication since childhood.
I want to create, create, and create.

A SMALL BOAT

I left a boat on the Neuse,
in the middle of the broad river.
Now fish no longer swim freely;
the river divides here, up and down,
while the distant hills no longer look wild.

It is a boat made of fiberglass,
moored in the waves
so birds passing by can rest on it,
knowing it's not an island
or a floating secret.

The forests and grassland on the banks
shift, as if to form
a new rhythm with the boat,
though it's not something
that will stay long on the Neuse.

CHOICE OF HOMETOWN

It's so easy for you
to choose your hometown,
a city where I am a refugee.
You want to take root here
and stop wandering with me.

You are already grown
and probably know I'm close to
my journey's end – from now on
I might move only in place.
I once thought you would be like me
sailing out for another sea,
but now you have your own coast,
unwilling to depart anymore.

I never imagined that I, rootless,
could give you root.
Perhaps it's unavoidable that
this generation scrambles through hardships
just to provide the next generation
with choices and hopes.

Indeed, every hometown
was once foreign to one's ancestors.
I remember a wise man saying,
"Blessed are those who have never left home
to open space for their children
and who can live and die in the same place
without needing a story
or exposing themselves to injury."

WHETHER YOU LIKE IT OR NOT

There are many things,
whether you like them
or not, that you must do.
Even your birth proved
a kind of reluctance.
Your parents were having great fun
but got carried away,
and soon your mother found
herself pregnant. Then they argued
for a long time about whether to keep
the baby. They changed
their minds back and forth,
but finally decided
to allow you into this world.

Don't work yourself up.
What I said is absolutely true.
If you don't believe me
you can go ask your mother.
Actually, you shouldn't be too concerned.
There's no need to find out
whether you were an accident
who threw your parents into a crisis.
What's essential is that they chose
the effort to raise you and let their love
for you enfold themselves
body and soul, and let your existence
define the boundary
of their happiness and stress.

Don't talk again about having your own way.
You must do what you should do,
whether you like it or not.

THE LOST MOON

Like you, I too lost my moon.
Wide-eyed, I took a smiling face
to be the source of all light and hope
which led me into a gloomy forest.
Since then, I can no longer see
the wonders in the sky.
However hard I trudge and search,
I cannot find the hills I have climbed.

Now, there's no difference between day and night
– I spend them on my computer and cell phone.
In fact, I knew long ago that
the smiling face was a mere mirage,
yet I can no longer gaze up at the moon
as my ancestors did
from horseback by the roadside
to relay a word home or to a friend.

I have landed in a place
my ancestors never heard of –
I need to grow a new backbone.

Echoes from Far Away

THE CAGE

I used to have a beautiful cage
that flew around day and night.
Its door opened and closed
showing how comfortable
and safe it was inside –
I should ride it through the clouds,
accepting the space within the cage
and working hard with others
to carry out a common dream.
That way, I could live an easy life
and leave behind many types of praise,
although I would have no other story.

Like a colored cloud, the cage
has wheeled around for decades.
It still looks gorgeous, like new,
but I am fully grown, too big
to get into it anymore.
I can board it only in my dreams.

ALL YOU HAVE IS A COUNTRY

You are so poor that all you have is a country.
Whenever you open your mouth
you talk about the country
to which you can no longer return.
China is a giant shield that you use
to conceal your cowardice and to preempt
the onslaught of duties and hardships.

You dare not take these as your rights:
the warm sunlight, clean water, fresh air,
a happy mood for an ordinary day.
As long as you live, you want to grieve
for the fairy tale of patriotism.

You dare not take a country as a watchdog –
a good dog wags its tail to please its master,
becomes fierce in deterring burglars;
a bad dog ignores invaders
and only bites and barks at its master.
You dare not clasp the dog's ear,
telling it, "You won't have food
if you continue to misbehave like this."

Actually, you are merely a grain of rice
that fell through China's teeth,
but you treat it as your god,
your universe, and the source
of your suffering and happiness.

THE OLDER GENERATION

I saw how they lived with restrictions.
Hardly past thirty they began to decline.
Like fish trapped in an invisible net,
they swam in all directions
but couldn't get anywhere.

They had to surrender to the country
and let it consume them at will.
They were like trees dependent
on the strength of the forest, but none
could stand tall and straight alone.

Their dreams were banished into caves
and withered away, never able to sprout.
While alive, they tried hard
to garner praise from everyone
so as to become model ghosts afterward.

THE LAST WISH

He used to be a lyric poet
and was well known all over the country
when he was not yet thirty.

Then he was selected by the state
to serve as a cultural official.
Everything was in order:
he didn't have to go to work on weekdays,
when he went out he used a chauffeur,
his job was handled by a secretary
except for the endless meetings he had to attend.
He lived in safety and privilege.
But for nearly half a century
he hasn't written a poem to his satisfaction,
though he is still called "China's Rilke."

Now he is dying.
His superiors are at his bedside,
offering him solicitous words
and asking whether he has some unfulfilled wish.
Suddenly he bursts into tears,
wailing, "I want to write poetry.
I want to leave you some immortal lines!"

A CABINET

There's a cabinet you'd better avoid.
Whoever has seen its contents
will get in trouble
and might risk prison.

The cabinet has never been locked.
It contains nothing but trifles:
drug prescriptions, conflicting orders,
banquet menus, assorted receipts,
notes of meetings, lists of familiar names.

These things are simply piled together.
Seeing them shouldn't be a crime,
but at any moment the cabinet door
might display such words:
NATIONAL SECRETS!

CONCRETENESS AND CLARITY

You pointed at my face and said, "How
could you let one person's memory
embody a billion people's experience?
This is like letting a dot represent
a vast surface – a distorted reality!"

A billion is a huge number.
Even Einstein
might be wary of it.
What do a billion faces look like?
How do a billion voices sound?
Not able to hear or see clearly,
you would have a head stuffed with clouds –
there'd be the same story for everyone.

Give me solidity and clarity.
Let me see one face, then another;
let me hear one voice, then another.
Big numbers can produce
only confusion and fraudulence.

INCOMPATIBLE

You often tell children:
"The world is what it is.
If you cannot change it,
you'd better get used to it."

What kind of logic is that?
To live, one must accept diminishment –
if sunlight is blocked out,
your eyes must adapt to the gloom;
if smog is too thick to disperse,
your lungs should breathe partially;
if fake foods are everywhere,
your stomach must grow stronger.
In any event, people all live the same way.

If the world continued like that,
humans would diminish by the generation,
regressing to animals, eventually
to plants and stones.

All progress starts with incompatibility –
people try to change their surroundings
to make conditions fit themselves.
Drop your adaptability
and let children learn
to become incompatible.

HANDS

When you're back in Beijing,
tell him I understand his situation
and won't contact him directly.
There are hands around him
that are always busy searching through
websites and emails and blogs.
They open letters and parcels
and record one name after another.
Sometimes they tap out hints
that startle sleepers and make them brood
about dangers until daybreak.

Tell him to be careful,
not to contact me unless necessary.
Those hands have eyes all over them,
able to monitor
countless people at once.
At any moment they can reach out
to seize you and dump you into
a canyon, or dungeon, or cavern.
Your cries for help
will elicit no response –
the ears on those hands can play deaf.

A CENSOR'S TALK

When you are in that country
you must spread the good news about us
and praise our marvelous land:
here children all enjoy free education,
the old are cared for, the sick treated,
people live and work happily,
united in social harmony.
You can say our life is sweeter than honey
(although there're a few lost ones
who squander public money for debauchery).
Moreover, our economy grows by the day.
Now it's so easy to travel and communicate.
This country is rich and vast,
a garden of bliss in every way.

When you return from that country
you must bring back their bad news:
people there all live miserable lives,
most families are deep in debt,
men drink excessively and carry arms,
women are loose and shameless,
citizens burn their national flag in the open
and even curse their president on television,
children cannot see the purpose of life,
abuse drugs and indulge in sex,
many young girls get pregnant and some give birth,
common people have no chance to excel,
their economy has kept declining
and will soon collapse.

Don't smirk like that.
I know what's on your mind.
You've been thinking how to emigrate

so you can live in that country for good.
If so, you'd better shut up.
And don't come back.

DO NOT START

You'd have to commit new violence to salvage
the wreckage left by the previous violence.
In this way you would produce new hatred until
hatred is everywhere, as thick as smog.

You'd have to tell a bigger lie
to cover up the previous lie.
In this way lies expand and multiply,
becoming huge like
a mountain or a country.

There are things that, once you start,
can drain your humanity.

IF EATING IS A CULTURE

We eat mice.
Mice have nice glossy fur
and can give you a head of thick hair.
Even if you're bald
they can restore your hair.

We eat cats.
Cats, quick by nature,
can make you smarter,
or at least livelier.

We eat frogs.
Frogs can swim and crow loudly.
They can make your voice resonant.
Even in the rainy season
you won't develop rheumatism.

We eat foxes.
Foxes are cunning and swift
and can increase your agility
in dodging traps laid for you.

We eat tigers.
Tigers, powerful and fierce,
can strengthen your body
and enhance your potency.
They can help you conquer
and dominate anywhere.

We eat phoenixes and dragons
but cannot catch them throughout
heaven and earth and ocean.

So we eat snakes for dragons
and chickens for phoenixes
so that we can eat them up as well.

WEASELS

In those days weasels often hexed villagers,
bewitching young girls
and women of frail health.
Such a victim would rave in a weasel's voice,
trembling and brandishing her arms.
Her family would rush out,
shouting and beating a basin
to scare away the weasel casting the spell.
Some carried brooms
to thrash the creature if they found it.
Once the rascal fled
the crazed person would return to calm.

Nowadays no one believes
that animals can hex humans.
Instead we send the possessed
to a shrink or hospital.
Sorcery is nothing but superstition.
Yet if a voice cries,
"Go chase the weasel away!"
I might hurry out to search through
haystacks, bushes, firewood
in hopes of finding a weasel
shrieking and rocking in spasms.

O WIND

O wind, tear up this heaven of clouds,
toss them out of the sky,
empty the space so the smog around us
might lift and disappear.

O wind, this city is expecting you
to send over a torrential rain
that can cleanse the dusty roofs,
can wash the streets shiny again,
can restore green to treetops,
can stop feverish vehicles from
honking and rushing around.

O wind, let seawater surge over the beach.
Let it take away piles of trash,
returning blue to the bay,
allowing fish scales to glitter again
on the crests of waves.

MY CHINA DREAM

I dream of becoming a scar on China's face,
because when it was moaning and bleeding
I, too, trembled in spasms.
When it was weeping, I was
also drenched in tears.
Its pain throbs in my soul
and through me, reaches numerous people.

I dream of becoming a scar on China's face.
When banners and praises are everywhere
I see intrigues in splendid disguise
and hear sighs and cries far away.
I am a mass of records
solidified by crimes and sufferings,
also by the denuded land.

However brightly China smiles,
I won't share its honor
or embellish its beauty,
though I often think how
I might fade away eventually.

A Quiet Center

DOORS

So many doors close once you pass them.
Don't turn around to trace back
the way you came, because
no matter how you shout or weep,
those doors won't budge a bit.

So many doors bang shut
the moment you cross them.
They propel you into dark corridors.
You have to move ahead, assuming
there might be a patch of light somewhere.

So many doors disappear
as soon as you leave them behind,
although voices keep reminding you:
Don't forget where you are from –
those doors lead to your roots.

You have gone through so many doors
and learned to lock them with ease.
If necessary, you will throw away
the keys you are supposed to keep.
You are used to finding your way.

ACCEPTANCE

In many people's eyes
absence is a fault or crime.
However hard you try to make amends,
they will still condemn you.
You can't go home anymore
and will drift on the wind of chance –
wherever you land
you will be an outsider.

Then, accept the role of wanderer.
At least you can stand alone
and become one of those
who live and die on their own.

You must learn to be content
to inhabit your own space –
news from far away
can no longer disturb you.
If necessary, turn your back on the past
and let all slander and praise
vanish from your mind.

ALONE

You don't know how fond I am of being alone.
The soul loves ancient guests from far away,
but they arrive only when you are alone.
Don't say it's hard to stand loneliness.
Wherever you are, in a village or on an island,
you won't lack divine friends
as long as you don't step out your door.

You don't know how I hate networking.
Banquets of a dozen courses
and endless parties cannot shrink
the distances between people.
The noise keeps you from hearing the voices of old,
and you make "siblings" randomly.
You don't know how happy I am when alone.

A CENTER

You must hold your quiet center,
where you do what only you can do.
If others call you a maniac or a fool,
just let them wag their tongues.
If some praise your perseverance,
don't feel too happy about it –
only solitude is a lasting friend.

You must hold your distant center.
Don't move even if earth and heaven quake.
If others think you are insignificant,
that's because you haven't held on long enough.
As long as you stay put year after year,
eventually you will find a world
beginning to revolve around you.

MISUNDERSTANDING

So let misunderstanding spread.
It only shows how different
you are from others.
Many things cannot bear
explaining; you'd better
let silence and labor speak
in your defense.

You don't need many friends
or to be enamored with beautiful women
or share the wine of happy gatherings,
because you have solitude enough,
content to leave this world without a sound.

Distant thunder can give you pure joy.
Birds in the sky can teach you
another kind of wisdom.
As your soul is growing new wings
such words will disappear from your dictionary:
boundary, complaint, cowardice, collapse ...

AT LEAST

You don't need to appear everywhere,
attending parties and conferences randomly.
That would show you are still
diffident about your art
and would also debase you.

People who see you in person
might think you're too common,
your achievement due to luck
like a blind cat that stumbles on a dead mouse.

Your frequent appearance
would dishearten others
because you exist far away,
at the end of their imagination –
you should be watched but not reached.

Look, this skyful of stars,
which one of them
doesn't shine or die alone?
Their light also comes
from a deep indifference.

PRAYER

Straighten up, my soul.
Don't try to please anyone alive.
Don't make way for any group.
Don't listen to sarcasm and hatred.

May you again burn with youthful madness.
Let your dream spread its rugged wings
so you won't weigh the odds when taking off,
and every flight will be your final one.

May you possess an animal-like disposition –
never complain or lose heart.
Live patiently like a bird or fish
and spend every day as your best one.

May you pursue ancient wisdom,
love truth more than beauty,
stay the course no matter how rough.
Let life and work be one.

May you become your own monument.

OLD

In no time you have become an old man.
Children on streets call you "granduncle."
You are old, really old.
You used to burn with so many desires,
consumed by bitterness and despair,
all because you wanted what did not belong to you.
You used to squander your life
hoping your soul's fire could light up
some eyes and dispel
one patch of darkness after another.

Now you are old,
but may your heart get purer,
burning only for one person or one thing
until it turns to ashes.

PAPER

You must cherish the blank paper in front of you
and write out words that cannot be erased.
If you are fortunate
they will keep a story evergreen
and will enter into your backbone.

This piece of paper is a humble beginning,
but no calumny, no power
can shake your words in black and white.
Your voice and timeless news
will rise from here gradually.
You must give all you have
to the good paper in front of you.

ACKNOWLEDGMENTS

I am grateful to these journals, in which the following poems originally appeared:

Narrative: "Acceptance," "At Least," "A Center," "The Detached," "The Lost Moon," and "My China Dream"

Poetry: "Missed Time"

ABOUT THE AUTHOR

Ha Jin left China for America in 1985. He writes in both English and Chinese. In English, he has published three previous volumes of poetry, eight novels, four collections of stories, and a book of essays. His work has been translated into more than thirty languages. He is a professor of English and creative writing at Boston University and lives outside Boston.

Lannan Literary Selections

For two decades Lannan Foundation has supported the publication and distribution of exceptional literary works. Copper Canyon Press gratefully acknowledges their support.

LANNAN LITERARY SELECTIONS 2018

Sherwin Bitsui, *Dissolve*

Jenny George, *The Dream of Reason*

Ha Jin, *A Distant Center*

Aimee Nezhukumatathil, *Oceanic*

C.D. Wright, *Casting Deep Shade*

RECENT LANNAN LITERARY SELECTIONS FROM
COPPER CANYON PRESS

Josh Bell, *Alamo Theory*

Marianne Boruch, *Cadaver, Speak*

Olena Kalytiak Davis, *The Poem She Didn't Write and Other Poems*

Michael Dickman, *Green Migraine*

John Freeman, *Maps*

Deborah Landau, *The Uses of the Body*

Maurice Manning, *One Man's Dark*

Rachel McKibbens, *blud*

W.S. Merwin, *The Lice*

Camille Rankine, *Incorrect Merciful Impulses*

Roger Reeves, *King Me*

Paisley Rekdal, *Imaginary Vessels*

Brenda Shaughnessy, *So Much Synth*

Richard Siken, *War of the Foxes*

Frank Stanford, *What About This: Collected Poems of Frank Stanford*

Ocean Vuong, *Night Sky with Exit Wounds*

Javier Zamora, *Unaccompanied*

Ghassan Zaqtan (translated by Fady Joudah), *The Silence That Remains*

Poetry is vital to language and living. Since 1972, Copper Canyon Press has published extraordinary poetry from around the world to engage the imaginations and intellects of readers, writers, booksellers, librarians, teachers, students, and donors.

WE ARE GRATEFUL FOR THE MAJOR SUPPORT PROVIDED BY:

THE PAUL G. ALLEN
FAMILY FOUNDATION

Anonymous

Jill Baker and Jeffrey Bishop

Donna and Matt Bellew

John Branch

Diana Broze

Sarah and Tim Cavanaugh

Janet and Les Cox

Mimi Gardner Gates

Linda Gerrard and Walter Parsons

Gull Industries, Inc.
on behalf of Ruth and William True

The Trust of Warren A. Gummow

Steven Myron Holl

Phil Kovacevich and Eric Wechsler

Lakeside Industries, Inc.
on behalf of Jeanne Marie Lee

TO LEARN MORE ABOUT UNDERWRITING
COPPER CANYON PRESS TITLES,
PLEASE CALL 360-385-4925 EXT. 103

WE ARE GRATEFUL FOR THE MAJOR SUPPORT PROVIDED BY:

Maureen Lee and Mark Busto

Rhoady Lee and Alan Gartenhaus

Ellie Mathews and Carl Youngmann as The North Press

Anne O'Donnell and John Phillips

Petunia Charitable Fund and advisor Elizabeth Hebert

Suzie Rapp and Mark Hamilton

Jill and Bill Ruckelshaus

Cynthia Lovelace Sears and Frank Buxton

Kim and Jeff Seely

Catherine Eaton Skinner and David Skinner

Dan Waggoner

Austin Walters

Barbara and Charles Wright

The dedicated interns and faithful volunteers
of Copper Canyon Press

The Chinese character for poetry is made up of two parts: "word" and "temple." It also serves as pressmark for Copper Canyon Press.

The interior is set in ITC Bodoni™ Twelve Book. Book design by VJB/Scribe. Printed on archival-quality paper using soy-based inks.